52 WEEKS
OF FAMILY
ITALIAN

Eileen Mc Aree

CONTENTS

Introduction

Learning a foreign language is a wonderful goal, and it can also be a fun and rewarding experience. What stops many people from attempting to learn a foreign language is their own fear of speaking, of looking foolish in front of another person. They may be comfortable studying vocabulary lists or grammar rules, but without actually speaking a language, no one can really progress. *52 Weeks of Family Italian* is designed to get you speaking Italian from the very first day!

Not only will you build on your own success as you learn to communicate in Italian, you will take your children along on this exciting journey. Children are naturally curious and full of enthusiasm. They haven't yet faced a conjugated verb or a double negative. They have no idea that learning to speak a foreign language is supposed to be difficult. What better study partners could you ask for? For most of us, our inhibitions about pronouncing foreign words disappear when we practice with our children. Using the simple lessons provided in this book, you and your children will be speaking to each other (and hopefully other people) in Italian quickly and easily.

52 Weeks of Family Italian is designed to be a relaxed, self-teaching guide. Each week you focus on a simple conversational concept that you and your children can practice together. The conversations were chosen based on their relevance to real, everyday family life. The lessons are short and simple and will get you and your family practicing Italian in the many of the moments modern families share together: mealtimes, morning "rush hour", carpools, bedtime. This is an oral introduction to the Italian language, so there are no spelling rules to memorize or flashcards to flip. Grammar is touched on throughout the curriculum but the main goal is to get you and your family speaking this beautiful language.

Features of the Book

Before you begin, take a look through the book. There are several features that will make the learning process easier for both you and your children.

- ## Words and Phrases to Get You Started
  This is a small compilation of some words and phrases you should know from the beginning to encourage and instruct your children.

- ## 52 Week Curriculum

  This is the heart of it all, and when you see how simple each week's lesson is, you may be surprised. Certain weeks focus on only one phrase! The fact is that fifty-two small, achievable lessons add up to quite a store of conversational skills, and conversation is the ultimate goal of this book. It was written to provide a family with a respectable oral vocabulary in about a year. Exactly how fast your family progresses is entirely up to you. If you and your kids are in a groove and you want to move ahead, by all means follow the momentum. On the other hand, if you are dealing with an ear infection, an impending dance recital and a huge deadline at work, stretch one week's lesson into three weeks. The pace is yours to decide. You and your family will be successful if you simply keep talking.

- ## Suggested Activities

As every busy parent knows, it is not always easy to find time to go to the supermarket, let alone learn *and teach* a brand new language. This section is full of realistic, fun and engaging ways to practice your Italian skills in the context of your everyday life.

- ## Resources

Listed here are many wonderful materials available to make learning a foreign language fun and engaging. The internet makes it possible to access many educational games for free. For those with "smart" phones, there are apps that can reinforce language learning while you wait outside school, in a fast food pick up line, or entertain a younger sibling at baseball practice. Also listed here are some books and CD's that can further pique your child's interest in the Italian language.

How to Use This Book

1. **52 Weeks of Family Italian** follows an auditory and oral learning model. Listening to the sounds of a new language and communicating successfully in that language opens the mind to a new structure of thinking. Vocabulary drills and grammar rules shut down the learning process at this early stage. This is not to imply vocabulary and grammar are not crucial to the mastery of any language. It is simply that to get the process started, *the natural way is to start talking.*

2. **Talk, Talk, Talk!** Use your new vocabulary every day, even it is only for a one minute conversation. You will be surprised and pleased to see how a minimal time commitment, *every day*, leads to the attainment of a great deal of vocabulary.

3. **Watch your pronunciation.** Try to correct any major pronunciation errors as soon as they occur. The pronunciation guides should help you with this. The faster you correct yourself, the faster you will learn.

4. **Touch on each week's** *cultural note.* Every week's lesson includes a facet of Italian life. Introducing children to Italian culture increases their curiosity about the language. It makes the process more interesting and fun for you as well!

5. **Take time to review**. Review weeks are built into the curriculum. Take your time! If you feel you and your family haven't mastered one week's concept, continue your review till you are ready to move on.

6. **Remember, it's a journey, not a race**. Many language courses advertise mastery of a language in record time. Babies don't learn to talk overnight, and people don't speak new languages overnight either. Your Italian speaking skills will continue to improve as long as you keep speaking and learning. Enjoy!

Suggested Activities

1. **Short and sweet conversations**. Each week's lesson is bite size Italian concept that you can review during a five minute conversation. Resist the impulse to drill, if your child forgot a word, just provide it for them. The repetition of language will help their vocabulary grow. Great places for bite-sized conversations are:

    - In the car…all parents spend plenty of time in the car! Use this time to squeeze in some language learning.
    - At mealtimes…many of the lessons in this book are perfect to review before breakfast, lunch or dinner…or snack at the pool…or a snack in the mall…..
    - Bedtimes…start with "Ti amo" and move on from there!
    - "Downtime"…Waiting in the pediatrician's examination room, waiting for your food to be delivered at Chili's, anytime or place you need to kill five minutes, use it to review Italian!

2. **Put on the radio.** By putting on Italian language CD or podcast in the car or kitchen while you make dinner, you acclimate your ear, and your children's if they are listening, to the rhythm and cadence of Italian speech. You are

hearing native or fluent speakers provide an accent model as well.

3. **Find an Italian language children's TV show.** Children's television shows are not terribly complicated in terms of character and plot, and you can derive meaning just by watching. Many familiar children's television shows are available online in Italian.

4. **Read a bilingual storybook.** The Resources section of this book lists websites that can help you locate children's picture books in both English and Italian. The plots are simple so you can get a lot of meaning from the picture clues. Also, reading aloud to your children helps you work on your accent.

5. **Say hello!** One of the hardest parts of learning a new language is overcoming our own embarrassment and communicating with native speakers. If you can get over this hurdle you will have conquered a challenge that turns many people away from learning a second language. In certain areas of the world, it may be easy to meet Italian speaking people. In others, it is difficult to find anyone who speaks Italian at all. Utilize the internet to locate groups of fellow Italian speakers.

6. **Make friends.** One of the benefits of learning about a new culture and language is meeting new friends. Whether you meet a local mother who hails from Rome or you need to utilize the internet to find language partners, you will surely enrich your life with the new and interesting people you will meet.

7. **Start a playgroup.** If you are a take charge kind of person, start your own playgroup! No matter where in the world you live, you can guarantee there are other parents

interested in teaching their children Italian. Internet sites like Meetup.com are great tools for creating playgroups.

8. **Play.** Have fun with Italian. The Resources section lists lots of fun games, books and CD's to support your learning. In addition, try playing the following vocabulary review games with your kids:

- *Dove si trova?* Ask your children where different items in the room are. They recognize the vocabulary word and point to the item.

- *Caldo o freddo?* This is your basic game of hot or cold except instead of hiding an object in the room, you *think* of an item in the room. You then direct your children toward it with cues of *caldo o freddo.* The child who figures out which item you were thinking of (lamp, television, etc.) must call out the name of the item in Italian.

- *Mamma (Papà) dice che toccare..."* Here is a version of Simon says. Mommy (or Daddy) says to touch different body parts, items in the room, items of clothing etc. Children must understand the vocabulary they are hearing in order to act accordingly. They are out if they touch something and Mama didn't say!

- *Venti Domande.* Children are given the opportunity to ask twenty questions to figure out the item you are thinking of. They can ask questions about it in English (or Italian as their knowledge increases) but they have to guess what it is in Italian.

- *Vedo qualcosa...* Play this game the same way you would play *I Spy.* As your vocabulary increases you can use more and more Italian describing words to help your children puzzle out what you see.

- ***Puppets.*** Puppets are an invaluable tool for teaching language. Buy or make a hand puppet, name your puppet (Try Italian names to go with your theme!), and make the puppet your Italian teacher's helper. Anytime you want to review dialog, take out your puppet and talk away. Older children can help put on the puppet show for younger children.

- ***Beanbag Toss***. This is simply another way to review vocabulary. Get a beanbag (or soft, small ball, or stuffed animal, anything that won't go through a window or cause a concussion). The first person says a word or phrase in Italian and tosses the beanbag to the next person who then has to give the translation. If they don't get the correct answer, they are out. If they do get the correct answer, they come up with another Italian phrase and toss the beanbag to the next person. You can reverse this activity and say the words or phrases in English and have the children provide the Italian translation. That is always a little harder!

Words and Phrases to Get You Started

As an individual, you are embarking on a journey to learn Italian. As a parent, you are additionally taking on the role of teacher. With this knowledge in mind, prepare yourself from day one with some basic vocabulary that will guide and encourage your children. It also adds to the language they will pick up through exposure!

Benissimo!:	Very good!
Fantastico!:	Fantastic!
Meraviglioso!:	Wonderful!
Dimmelo di nuovo:	Tell me again.
Ripeti, per favore:	Repeat, please.
Prova ancora:	Try again.
Sta attento!:	Pay attention!
Calmati :	Calm down.
Aspetta :	Wait.
Vieni qui:	Come here.
Buon lavoro! :	ood job!
Ascoltami :	Listen to me.
In un secondo…:	In a second….
And don't forget……*Ti amo :*	I love you!

52 Week Curriculum

Here is an overview of how the weeks of your year of learning Italian are divided. Topics were chosen for ease of learning and application to real life. Suggested reviews are included in each week's lesson. Don't feel compelled to go in order! If you want to learn how to say, "I'm hungry!" in Italian, by all means skip straight to Unit 5. Remember, go in an order that is interesting to you and at a speed you and your family are comfortable with. This book was written to make Italian learning easy and fun!

Unit 1: Weeks 1-8
Theme: Making Friends
Cultural Spotlight: Introducing Italy

Unit 2: Weeks 9-16
Theme: All About Me
Cultural Spotlight: A Child's Life in Italy

Unit 3: Weeks 17-24
Theme: Welcome to My Home
Cultural Spotlight: Italian Art and Music

Unit 4: Weeks 25-32
Theme: Useful Information
Cultural Spotlight: Italian Food

Unit 5: Weeks 33-40
Theme: Mealtimes
Cultural Spotlight: Famous Italian People

Unit 6: 41-48
Theme: Getting Ready
Cultural Spotlight: Italian Culture Around the World

Unit 7: Weeks 49-52
Theme: A Few Odds and Ends
Cultural Spotlight: Fun Italian Facts!

Unit 1: Making Friends

Week 1: Manners

Vocabulary:

sì/no *see/noh*	(yes/no)
prego *preh-goh*	(please)
grazie *grah-tsyeh*	(thanks)
grazie mille *grah-tsyeh-mee-leh*	(thank you very much)
non c'e di che *nohn-cheh-dee-keh*	(you're welcome)

Pronunciation note: The vowel sounds in Italian differ widely from the vowel sounds in English. Try to listen to spoken Italian to hear the differences.

A: sounds like *ah*, as in father.

U: sounds like *oo* in boot.

I: sounds like *ee*, as in feet.

E: can be pronounced two ways: An open e sound, *eh*, like in met or a closed e sound, *ay* like it fate.

O: can be pronounced two ways as well. An open o sound, *aw*, like in thaw, or a closed o sound, like *oh*, in boat.

Cultural Note: Have you ever looked at a map of Europe and seen a country shaped like a boot? That country is Italy! Italy is surrounded on three sides by water, the Mediterranean Sea and the Adriatic Sea.

Idea! Use your new manners words at mealtimes. Pair the English word of whatever you want with the Italian manners word. Encourage your children to do the same. Don't worry about mixing up the languages, that's how communication is born.

Week 2: Greetings

Review: Week 1: Manners

Vocabulary:

    ciao   (hello)
    chow

    arrivederci   (goodbye)
    ah-ree-veh-dehr-chee

    buongiorno   (Good morning)
    buh-ohn-johr-noh

    buonasera   (Good evening)
    buh-oh-nah-seh-rah

Pronunciation note: Sometimes in Italian, the letters are written but remain silent. Remember to drop the i in *ciao*.

Cultural Note: The top of Italy's "boot" is bordered by the Alps, the tallest mountain range in Europe.

Idea! Make your goodbyes in the morning Italian. Kids will get a kick out of telling you, *Arrivederci!,* before they get on the bus.

Week 3: Introductions

Review: Week 2: Greetings

Vocabulary:

Come state?   Come sta?   (How are you)
koh-meh-stah-teh   koh-meh-stah

Sto bene   (good)
Stoh – beh-neh

E Lei?   (and you?)
eh- lehy

Grammar note:. Use *Come state?* to ask, "How are you?" to more than one person. Use the formal form, *Come sta*? to ask, "How are you?" to one person (adult).

Cultural Note: Rome is one of the oldest and most beautiful cities in the world. You can still see the ruins of Ancient Rome scattered throughout the city. Rome's nickname is, "The Eternal City".

Idea! Have fun role playing out a simple conversation with your children.

Buongiorno. Come state?/Come sta?

Sto bene, grazie. E Lei?

Bene, grazie.

Week 4: What's Your Name?

Review: Week 2: Greetings

Vocabulary:

Come si chiama?/ Come ti chiami?   (What is your name ?)
Koh-meh-see-kyah-mah / koh-meh-tee-kyah-mee

Mi chiamo_____.   (My name is_____.)
mee-kyah-moh_____.

Grammar note: There is a formal your, *si*, and an informal you, *ti*, in Italian. If you were asking an adult their name, you would use *si*. If you were asking a child, you would use *ti*.

Cultural note: The Ancient Ruins of Rome are more than 2000 years old! People come from all over the world to see the Forum, the Pantheon and the Colosseum.

Idea! Velvet rope your kitchen! Before dinner or other mealtime where you are not too rushed, hang a streamer across the kitchen door and before children can enter they must answer the question, *"Come ti chiami?"*.

Week 5: How Old Are You?

Review: Week 4: What is Your Name?

Vocabulary:

Quanti anni hai?   (How old are you?)
kwahn-tee-ah-nee-I

Io ho_____anni.   (I am ____ years old.)
Ih-yoh-oh_____ah-nee

Pronunciation note: The letter "h" in Italian is never spoken. Read *hai* like I in English.

Cultural Note: Mt. Vesuvius is a volcano that looms over the city of Naples. Thousands of years ago, the volcano erupted and buried the towns of Pompeii and Herculaneum. You can visit those ancient towns today and see what life what life in an Italian village thousands of years ago.

Idea! Teach your child the Italian number for their age. Then interview each other as if you just met using the vocabulary from the previous lessons. Siblings can interview each other!

Week 6: More Greetings

Review: Week 3, Introductions

Vocabulary:

Come va?	(How's it going?)
koh-meh-vah	
E tu?	(and you?)
eh-too	
A presto!	(See you soon!)
ah-preh-stoh	

Grammar note: In Italian, there is a formal and informal way to address others. In Week 2, you learned the formal way to greet neighbors, coworkers or the way children would address adults. *"Come va?"* is the more relaxed way of greeting one another. You could say this to friends or people you feel comfortable with. *Tu* is the informal way of saying you.

Cultural note: Grapes and olives are important crops in Italy. Many Italian farms are small family farms.

Idea! Incorporate these new phrases into your everyday life. *"Come va?"* can be used every day while checking to see how the kid's homework is coming along. *"A presto!"* is a great way to say goodbye before leaving for work in the morning.

Week 7: Nice to Meet You!

Review: Week 4: What's Your Name?

Vocabulary:

Piacere!   (It's nice to meet you!)
Pyah-cheh-reh

Grammar note: You can also say "*Molto lieto*"(*mohl-toh-lee-yeh-toh)* -masculine or "*Molto lieta*" (*mohl-toh-lee-yeh-tah*)- feminine to say, "It's nice to meet you!"

Cultural note: The currency of Italy is the Euro. Italy is a member of the European Union.

Idea! Let your family pretend they have never met. They can make up new names and ages. Let them experiment with the conversational phrases they learned in the last few weeks. Make sure they end their role play conversations with, *"Piacere!"*.

Week 8: Review

- **Review:** all basic conversational vocabulary.

    ○ Use dolls or puppets to role play introductions.

- It can be challenging in some parts of the world to find people with whom to speak Italian. Try posting a notice at your local library for Italian study buddies (children or adults!). You will see that there are Italian speakers located in every corner of the globe!

- Learn more about Italy:

    ○ Go to an Italian restaurant.
    ○ Read about the Roman Empire.
    ○ Go to a department store and search for Italian fashions. Italian designers are famous for their clothing and shoes.
    ○ Utilize the internet to "tour" some of the ancient sights of Italy.
    ○ Color in a Italian flag.
    ○ The Italians are avid sports fans. Watch an Italian soccer game online. The Italians have won the FIFA World Cup four times. Another exciting Italian sport to watch is Formula One Grand Prix racing.

Unit 2: All About Me

Week 9: Who Am I?

Review: Basic conversation from Week 1-8.
Vocabulary:

Chi sei tu?   (Who are you?)
kee-say- too

Sono una ragazza.   (I am a girl.)

Soh-noh-oo-nah-rah-gah-tsah

Sono un ragazzo.   (I am a boy.)

Soh-noh-oon-rah-gah-tsoh

Io sono _____.   (I am *insert child's name.*)

Ih-yoh-soh-noh_____.

Grammar note: When speaking Italian, words change depending on gender.

Here we use the article *una* when we are talking about a female or feminine object or *un'* (if the noun starts with an vowel- *un'amica*).

When we are talking about a male or masculine object we use the article *un* or *uno* (before some letters or groups of letters- *uno zio/uno studente)*.

Cultural note: School is free in Italy from preschool all the way through high school.

Idea! Take turns answering the question, *"Chi siete voi"*. Encourage your children to also use previously learned vocabulary (ex: it would also be appropriate to respond, Io mi chiamo_____). If your children would like to expand on the lesson, look up the translation of something he or she loves to do.

Examples: *"Io sono un ballerina"* : I am a dancer.

> *Ih-yoh-soh-noh-uhn-bah-leh-ree-noh*
> For a girl you would say: una ballerina
> *uh-nah-bah-leh-ree-nah*

> Remember to watch your use of gender!

Week 10: Feelings

Review: Week 3: Introductions
Vocabulary:

    Io sono felice.   (I am happy.)
    ih-yoh-soh-noh-feh-lee-cheh

    Io sono triste.   (I am sad.)
    ih-yoh-soh-noh-tree-steh

Cultural note: In Itay, schools are split up into three groups. The youngest students attend *scuola elementare* till they are about 11 years old. Then, the students begin *scuola secondaria di 1 grado,* which they attend till they are 16. If the student chooses to continue his education, he must take an exam and can then enter the *scuola secondaria superior.*

Idea! Have your children make exaggerated faces while they say in Italian whether they are happy or sad

Week 11: What Do I Look Like?

Review: Week 9: Who Am I?

Vocabulary:

Io sono *Ih-yoh-soh-noh*	(I am)
alto,-a *ahl-toh,-a*	(tall)
basso,-a *bah-soh,-a*	(short)
bello,-a *behl-oh, -a*	(pretty)
carino,-a *kah-ree-noh,-a*	(handsome)

Grammar note: Adjectives are typically presented with both the male and female endings. You decide which ending to use based on who or what you are describing.

Example:*Il ragazzo è alto.*   (The boy is tall.)

       La ragazza è alta   .(The girl is tall.)

Cultural note: Bocce ball is an Italian game many children are taught to play.

Idea! Use your cell phone to call your house phone. Let your kids chat to one another, greeting each other and describing themselves in Italian.

Week 12: What Do I Look Like?

Review: Week 11: What Do I Look Like?

Vocabulary:

Io ho i capelli biondi.　　(I have blond hair.)
Ih-yoh-oh-ih-kah-peh-lee-byohn-dee

Io ho i capelli bruni.　　(I have brown hair.)
Ih-yoh-oh-ih-kah-peh-lee-bruh-nee

Io ho i capelli rossi.　　(I have red hair.)
Ih-yoh-oh-ih-kah-peh-lee- roh-see

Io ho i capelli neri.　　(I have black hair.)
Ih-yoh-oh-ih-kah-peh-lee- neh-ree

Grammar note: Italian words have to match in gender and also in number. If you are talking about more than one noun, all the describing words attached to it must also show that it is more than one.

Cultural note: Family is very important to Italians. Many times, children may live with both their parents and grandparents. Italian children get a lot of loving attention from the whole family!

Idea! Have your children draw a self portrait. They can then use their new vocabulary to describe what they have drawn.

Week 13: What I Like to Do

Review: Weeks 11-12: What Do I Look Like?

Vocabulary:

> Che cosa ti piace fare?　　(What do you like to do ?)
> *Keh-koh-sah-tee-pyah-cheh-fah-reh*

> Mi piace leggere.　　(I like to read.)
> *mee-pyah-cheh-lejeh-reh*

> Mi piace nuotare　　(I like to swim.)
> *mee-pyah-cheh-nwoh-tah-reh*

Grammar note: Verbs are words that tell about things we can do. We add a verb to the phrase "*Mi piace*" to tell what we like to do.

Cultural note: Many Italian children learn their family business at a young age, and are expected to help out.

Idea! Have each child pick their own activity they like to do (not listed above). Help them look up the Italian verb online or in a Italian dictionary and make their own sentence. Suggestions: *ballare (to dance), cantare (to sing), giocare a calcio (to play soccer), giocare al computer (to play on the computer).*

Week 14: My Face

Review: Weeks 11 and 12: What Do I Look Like?:

Vocabulary:

Toccati il tuo/la tua/i tuoi/le tue...   (Touch your...)

Toh-kah-tee-ihl-two-oh/lah-two-ah/ih-two-oh-ee/leh-two-eh

(il) naso *ihl-nah-zoh*	(nose)
(il) viso *ihl-veeh-zoh*	(face)
(la) bocca *lah-boh-kah*	(mouth)
(gli) occhi *ly-oh-kee*	(eyes)
(le) orecchie *leh-oh-reh-kyeh*	(ears)

Grammar note: In Italian, when we use the word "your", we have to decide whether to be familiar or formal. Here we are using the familiar "your". However, you still have to match your pronoun "your" to the object's gender and number.

For this reason, You would say, *Toccati il tuo naso* (male, singular). *Toccati la tua bocca* (female, singular), and *Toccati i tuoi occhi* (plural).

Don't worry if you mix up your pronouns at this early stage of learning, but try and practice "matching" the right form of "your" with different parts of the face.

Cultural note: Many Italian children are named after a catholic saint and celebrate the saint's day in addition to their own birthday.

Idea! Play a version of "Simon Says" called "Mamma dice". This is a game you can play anywhere to review vocabulary. "Mamma dice: Toccati il tuo naso!" Remember, if Mamma didn't say…you are out!

Week 15: My Body

Review: Week 14: My Face

Vocabulary:

        (la) testa   (head)
        lah teh-stah

        (il) braccio   (arm)
        ihl-brah-choh

        (il) piede   (foot)
        ihl-pyeh-deh

        (la) gamba   (leg)
        lah-gahm-bah

        (la) mano   (hand)
        lah-mahn-oh

Cultural note: The children's story, *Pinnochio* was written in Italy by Carlo Collodi.

Idea! Expand on your "Mamma dice" game to include parts of the body.

Week 16: Review

- Review all vocabulary from the past eight weeks.

  - Role play conversations
  - Draw self portraits and describe
  - Point out other people and pretend to be them. How would they describe themselves?

- Learn more about Italian family life.

  - Make a family style dinner. Invite over your extended family and enjoy each other's company.
  - Go out for pizza!
  - Introduce your children to the original Pinnochio. Be aware, it is a little scarier than the Disney version.
  - Play *Lupo che oro sono?,* the Italian game of "What Time Is It Mr. Wolf?" One child is the wolf, who stands with his back to the other players, who are lined up across the room. The children call, *Lupo che oro sono?* and the wolf replies with a number. The children can then take that number of steps forward. The first child to the wolf can tag him and take their turn as the wolf. Look out though! The wolf may reply, *Ho fame!* (I'm hungry!) and turn and chase the kids back across the room! This is a great way to practice Italian vocabulary as well!

Unit 3: Welcome to My Home

Week 17: Welcome to My Home

Review: Weeks 9-16

Vocabulary:

> Benvenuti a casa mia!　　　(Welcome to my home!)
> *Behn-veh-nutee-ah-kah-sah-mee-yah*

Cultural note: The *Mona Lisa* is arguable the most famous painting of all time. It was painted by Leonardo da Vinci in the beginning of the sixteenth century. People are still trying to figure out what Mona Lisa was smiling about!

Idea! Take the plunge! Invite someone over, drum up your courage and welcome them in Italian. If you feel corny, don't worry. The more you use your Italian, the more natural it feels.

Week 18: Where Is It?

Review: Week 17: Welcome to my home!

Vocabulary:

Dov'è….. ?   (Where is……?)
Doh-veh

il bagno   (bathroom)
ihl-bah-nyoh

la cucina   (kitchen)
lah-koo-chee-nah

Grammar note: Remember, all Italian nouns are masculine or feminine. Is *il bagno* masculine or feminine? How about *la cucina*?

Cultural note: The ancient Romans were the first architects to make wide use of the arch. You can see examples of their use of the arch in many structures still standing today, including the Colosseum.

Idea! Practice using "Dov'è…?" with words you already know. This is a quick and easy way to practice.

"Dov'è (insert your child's name)?"

"Dov'è il tuo naso?"

Week 19: Where Is _____?

Review: Week 18: Where Is... ?

Vocabulary:

il tavolo   (table)
ihl-tah-voh-loh

la sedia   (chair)
lah-seh-dyah

la porta   (door)
lah-pohr-tah

la finestra   (window)
lah-fee-neh-strah

Cultural note: The Romans also utilized another architectural feature: the dome. You can see a dome in the Pantheon.

Idea! Have a treasure hunt! Hide some prizes (something small, an m&m, or sticker) in spots around your house. Say; "Dov'è il tavolo?" for example, and let your child claim the prize when they find the right object.

Week 20: Meet My Family (A)

Review: Week 19: Where is it?

Vocabulary:

> `Questo è mio padre.   (This is my father.)
> *kweh-stoh-eh-mee-yoh-pah-dreh*

> Questa è mia madre.   (This is my mother.)
> *kweh-stah-eh-mee-yah-mah-dreh*

Grammar note:. *Questo è/ Questa è* is a very important phrase as it can mean, "it is", "this is", or "that is" depending on the context of the sentence. Use *Questo è* for masculine nouns and *Questa è* for feminine nouns.

Cultural note: The statue of *David* by the famed sculptor Donatello depicts the hero form the ancient bible story David and Goliath.

Idea! At dinner let your kids have fun presenting their mom or dad.

Week 21: Meet My Family (B)

Review: Week 20: Meet My Family (A)

Vocabulary:

Chi è questo?   (Who is this?)
kee-eh-kweh-stoh

Questo è moi fratello.   (This is my brother.)
kweh-sto-eh-mee-yoh-frah-teh-loh

Questa è mia sorella.   (This is my sister.)
kweh-stah-eh-mee-yah-soh-reh-lah.

Pronunciation note: The letters "qu" is always pronounced like *kw.*

Cultural note: *La Bella* is a painting by Titian. It shows a beautiful Italian woman. Titian was a renowned painter from the Italian Renaissance.

Idea! Car practice: Have your children take turns "introducing" everyone in the car .

Week 22: Meet My Family (C)

Review: Weeks 20 and 21: Meet My Family (A and B)

Vocabulary:

la nonna	(grandmother)
lah-noh-nah	
il nonno	(grandfather)
ihl-noh-noh	
la zia	(aunt)
lah-tsee-yah	
lo zio	(uncle)
loh-tsee-yoh	
il cugino / la cugina	(cousin)
ihl-kuh-jee-noh/ lah-kuh-jee-nah	

Cultural note: Italian opera is considered by many to be the best in the world. Italy has produced some of the most talented opera singers the world has ever known.

Idea! Go through your family album and identify members of your family in Italian.

Week 23: His Name Is_____.

Review: Weeks 20-22: Meet My Family (A,B,C)

Vocabulary:

Io mi chiamo…	(My name is…)
Ih-yoh-mee-kyah-moh	
Lui si chiama	(His name is…)
luhy-see-kyah-mah	
Lei si chiama …	(Her name is…)
lehy-see-kyah-mah	

Grammar note: Sometimes the phrasing in another language is different than what we are used to in English. In , we are literally saying, "He is called…" or "She is called..". However, when learning a new language, always translate for meaning. In English we would phrase this as, "His name is….".

Cultural note: Since Italy has always been divided into many regions, folk misuc and dance have varied greatly within the country. One well known folk dance is the *Tarantella*.

Idea! Go around the dinner table and tell your own name and the name of the person on the right.

Week 24: Review

- Review vocabulary and concepts from weeks 17-23.

  - Now you have the phrases, " Toccati il tuo/la tua...." and "Dov'è...?" under your belt. These are two of the quickest ways to do impromptu reviews anywhere! Use them whenever you think of them.
  - Throw an old magazine in your car. When you have some wait time at pick ups or drop offs, ask kids to point to la finestra, la porta, etc
  - Have a camera phone or digital camera? Let your kids scroll through the pictures as long as they are verbally labeling all the family members they see.

- Learn more about the arts in Italy:

  - Get a book on the artists of the Italian Renaissance out from the library.
  - Look up images of the beautiful varied examples of Roman architecture.
  - Listen to a CD of Verdi's operas as you get dinner ready.
  - Watch Cecilia Bartolli perform on YouTube.
  - Read about the painting of the Sistine Chapel .
  - Download songs by Andreas Bocelli.

Unit 4: Useful Information

Week 25: Days of the Week

Review: Review Weeks 17-24

Vocabulary:

lunedì	(Monday)
luh-neh-dee	
martedì	(Tuesday)
mahr-teh-dee	
mercoledì	(Wednesday)
mehr-koh-leh-dee	
giovedì	(Thursday)
joh-veh-dee	
venerdì	(Friday)
veh-nehr-dee	
sabato	(Saturday)
sah-bah-toh	
domenica	(Sunday)
doh-meh-nee-kah	

Grammar note: The days of the week in Italian are not capitalized as they are in English.

Example: *Oggi è lunedì*. (Today is Monday.)

Oh-jee-eh-luh-neh-dee

Cultural note: Pasta is probably the most famous Italian dish. Depending upon where you travel in Italy, you will find different, delicious ways of preparing pasta.

Idea! Write the days of the week on index cards and put them all in an envelope. Let your children take turns taking out the correct day of the week and hanging it on the fridge with a magnet.

Week 26: What Day is Today?

Review: Week 25: Days of the Week

Vocabulary:

      Che giorno è oggi?   (What day is today?)
      keh-johr-noh-eh-oh-jee

Cultural note: Pizza is popular all over the world but it came from Italy! It got its start as a seasoned flatbread and evolved into the delicious dish we know today.

Idea! Ask your kids each morning before they start their day, *"Che giorno è oggi?"*

Week 27: Numbers 1-10

Review: Week 5: How Old Are You?

Vocabulary:

zero   (zero)
zeh-roh

uno   (one)
uh-noh

due   (two)
duh-eh

tré   (three)
treh

quattro   (four)
kwah-troh

cinque   (five)
cheen-kweh

sei   (six)
say

sette   (seven)
seh-teh

otto   (eight)
oh-toh

nove   (nine)
noh-veh

dieci   (ten)
dyeh-chee

Cultural note: Italians like to keep their breakfast, called *colazione,* simple. A coffee, or hot chocolate or hot milk for children, and bread and butter is a typical breakfast meal.

Idea! Use playing card to help kids memorize their numbers. Hold up a card and if the child says the correct number in Italian, they get to keep the card. Make the joker worth *zero* and the jack, queen and king worth *dieci.*

Week 28: How Many?

Review: Week 27: Numbers 0-10

Vocabulary:

Quanto?   (How many?)
Kwahn-toh

Grammar note: In order to be able to speak any language, you need to know key question words. Now you can add *quanto* to your existing repertoire of *che cosa, che, chi, dove* and *come*. You can get quite a lot of information with these simple words!

Cultural note: *Pranzo*, or lunch, is the most important meal of the day in Italy.

Idea! Review previous vocabulary through counting. *Quante finestre? Quanti ragazzi?*

Week 29: Months

Review: Week 25: Days of the Week

Vocabulary:

gennaio
jeh-nah-yoh
(January)

febbraio
feh-brah-yoh
(February)

marzo
mahr-tsoh
(March)

aprile
ah-pree-leh
(April)

maggio
mah-joh
(May)

giugno
juh-nyoh
(June)

luglio
luh-lyoh
(July)

agosto
ah-goh-stoh
(August)

settembre
seh-tehm-breh
(September)

ottobre
oh-toh-breh
(October)

novembre
noh-vehm-breh
(November)

dicembre   (December)
dee-chehm-breh

Grammar note: As you have probably noted from previous lessons, many words are the same in both Italian and English, just with different pronunciation. Other words are extremely similar. So you already know more Italian than you think!

Cultural Note: Many people in Italy have a mid-afternoon snack called a *merenda* to hold them till their late dinner.

Idea! Many Italian names for the months sound similar to their English counterparts. Use this similarity to help your kids memorize them. Give your children a clue and they have to guess the month you are talking about in English:

Clue: The flowers bloom in *maggio.* Answer: May

Clue: We fly kites in *marzo*. Answer: March

Week 30: I Know.....

Review: Weeks 25 & 29: Days and Months of the Year

Vocabulary:

Io so	(I know…)
ih-yoh-soh	
i giorni della settimana!	(the days of the week!)
ih-johr-nee-deh-lah-seh-tee-mah-nah	
i mesi dell'anno!	(the months of the year)
ih-meh-zee-dehl-ah-noh	

Pronunciation note: You have probably already noted the large number of double consonants in the Italian words you are learning. You have to accentuate them in pronunciation. Sometimes it is very important to accentuate the double consonants. Words can have different meanings considering the number of consonants. For example: *capelli* (with one "p") means hear and *cappelli* (with two "p") means hat.

Cultural note: *Cena*, or dinner, is held late, and is typically a lighter meal. Soup, salad, cold meats or pasta might be served.

Idea! Let your kids brag! Encourage them to tell Grandma, or their teacher, or friend that they know the days of the week and the months of the year. Every time they use their Italian to communicate (even to brag a little) they are learning more of the language!

Week 31: When Is Your Birthday?

Review: Week 29: Months of the Year

Vocabulary:

Quando è il tuo compleanno?   (When is your birthday?)
Kwahn-doh-eh-ihl-two-oh-kohm-pleh-ah-noh

Il mio compleaano è ….   (My birthday is in…..)
ihl-mee-yoh-kohm-pleh-ah-noh-eh

Grammar note: Here we are using the familiar form of your, *tuo*. You would probably know someone fairly well if you were asking them their birthday! If you were asking a teacher, for example, you would use the formal your, *Suo.(su-oh)*

Cultural note: Italian ice cream is called gelato.

Idea! If your child's birthday is between 1-10 let them try to figure out how they would say the date of their birth: *"Il mio compleanno è il 4 giugno"*. If their birthday is a bigger number, help them look up the number and figure it out!

Week 32: Review

- Learning all this useful information requires a lot of memorization.

  - Use playing cards or preschool counting flashcards to review numbers.
  - Count cars on the road. How many...trucks, red cars, motorcycles, etc.
  - Practice your days of the week song or create your own.
  - Try some fun games and videos available online. I like the games on digitaldialects.com/italian and bbc.co.uk/schools/primarylanguages/italian
  - Have a group birthday party. Bake tiramisu or another tasty Italian treat. Everyone has to state their birthday in order to get a taste.

- Learn more about the food of Italy

  - Try feeding your children an afternoon merenda.
  - Visit an Italian bakery.
  - Structure a dinner the Italian way, course by course.
  - Enjoy some pasta for dinner.
  - Introduce your child to polenta or risotto, also popular in sections of Italy.

Unit 5: Mealtimes

Week 33: I'm Hungry

Review: Concepts from Weeks 25-32

Vocabulary:

Hai fame?	(Are you hungry?)
I-fah-meh	

Ho fame.	(I'm hungry.)
oh-fah-meh	

Grammar note: Remember not to read the letter h. In Italian, when we answer a question in the negative, we just put the word *non* before the verb.

Example: *(Tu) hai fame?*   *No, non ho fame.*

Cultural note: Leonardo da Vinci was a painter, sculptor, mathematician and inventor during the sixteenth century. He created masterpieces that millions of people come to see even today.

Idea! This is one of the easiest conversations to practice because we all have meals every day! Incorporate this simple question into your regular mealtimes.

Week 34: Favorite Foods

Review: Week 33: I'm Hungry

Vocabulary:

il pane   (bread)
ihl- pah-neh

la mela   (apple)
lah- meh-lah

la marmellata   (jam)
lah-mahr-meh-lah-tah

il formaggio   (cheese)
ihl-for-mah-joh

i biscotti   (cookies)
ih-bee-skoh-tee

le carote   (carrots)
leh-kah-roh-teh

Pronunciation note: Remember to accentuate the double consonants like in *marmellata* or in *biscotti*.

Cultural note: Mario Andretti, is often referred to as "The Driver of the Century". He is the only racer to win the Indianapolis 500, the Formula One and Nascar championships.

Idea! Brainstorm your own list of favorite foods. Your kids will learn their own favorites quicker if they have to ask for them in Italian in order to receive them!

Week 35: I Like......

Review: Week 34: Favorite Foods

Vocabulary:

Vorresti..   (Do you like...?)
Voh-reh-stee...

Vorrei   (I like....)
Voh-rehy

Grammar note: *Vorresti* and *Vorrei* are two forms of the verb volere (irregular verb), which means, to like . In Italian, the verb changes depending on who or what it is referring to.

Cultural note: Luciano Pavarotti was one of the most famous opera singers of the 20th century. His vibrant personality is credited with making opera much more popular worldwide.

Idea! You can have a lot of fun practicing this concept. Tell the children they are having horrible things for breakfast, lunch, or dinner and innocently ask them, *"Vorresti questo?"* They can respond with an emphatic, *"No!"*

Week 36: I'm Thirsty!

Review: Week 33: I'm Hungry!

Vocabulary:

(Tu) Hai sete ?	(Are you thirsty?)
I-seh-teh	
(Io) Ho sete .	(I'm thirsty.)
oh-seh-teh	

Grammar note: The phrase, *"Hai sete?"* literally means *"Do you have thirst?"*. Similarly, *"Ho sete."* means, *"I have thirst."* This is yet another example of why we translate for meaning, not word for word.

Cultural note: Christopher Columbus is an Italian who discovered the New World on his trip in 1492.

Idea! A hot summer's day is a great time to make a pitcher of lemonade and see who is thirsty. Weather not warm? Try and make some hot cocoa instead!

Week 37: Can I Have......?

Review: Week 34: Favorite Foods

Vocabulary:

Vorrei.....per favore .   (I would like_____please?)
Voh-rehy-pehr-fah-voh-reh

Grammar note: As in English, there are more than one ways to request things in Italian. Just like in English, it is important to ask politely, adding *per favore*.

Cultural note: Michelangelo is the painter of the Sistine Chapel.

Idea! Make snack time practice time! Let your children pick their own afternoon *merenda* and then ask for it – *in italiano*-of course!

Week 38: Sit at the Table

Review: Week 37: Can I Have…?

Vocabulary:

> A tavolo! (Sit at the table.)
> *ah-tah-voh-loh*

Pronunciation note: *A tavolo* means "at the table".You can also say- *Siediti a tavolo*! to one person or *Sedetevi a tavolo! t*o more than one person. (*see-yeh-dee-tee-ah-tah-voh-loh/ seh-deh-teh-vee-ah-tah-voh-loh)*

Cultural note: Maria Montessori was a doctor at the turn of the twentieth century. She wanted to make education better for kids. Her methods are still used in schools today.

Idea! Assign a "dinner helper" who gets the rest of the family to the table each night. Pick a different dinner helper every night so each child gets a chance to practice using and listening to this command.

Week 39: Where Is My.....?

Review: Week 38: Sit Down at the Table.

Vocabulary:

la tazza *lah-tah-tsah*	(cup)
la forchetta *lah-for-keh-tah*	(fork
il coltello *ihl-kohl-teh-loh*	(knife)
il cucchiaio *ihl-cook-yah-yoh*	(spoon)
e *eh*	(and)

Pronunciation note: Remember the word *e* is pronounced like the *e* in English word end.

Cultural note: Giorgio Armani is a fashion designer. Men from every country want to wear suits designed by Armani.

Idea! Pair up different items you have previously learned using your new word *e*. Play *Mamma dice* with two items instead of one.

Example: *Mamma dice, "Toccati il tuo naso e la tua bocca".*

Week 40: Review

- Mealtime vocabulary is some of the easiest vocabulary to learn. Practice times occur every day so it feels easy and natural to incorporate these words. In addition, children enjoy learning and using the names of their favorite foods.

  - At a restaurant, see if you can translate any items on the menu.
  - Mix your old vocabulary with new. When asked, "Come va?" you can respond, "Io ho fame". You can use the phrase, "Dov'è …?" to locate food items on the table.

- Learn more about some famous Italian people!

  - Visit your local library and take out biographies on famous Italian citizens. There are too many to name!
  - Go to biography.com to find a wide selection of stories about men, women and children from Italy.

Unit 6: Getting Ready

Week 41: Wake Up!

Review: Vocabulary and concepts from weeks 32-39.

Vocabulary:

> Svegliati!   (Wake up!)
> *Zvehl-yah-tee*

> Buongiorno, figlio mio!   (Good morning ,my child!)
> *Buh-ohn-johr-noh-feel-yoh-mee-oh*

Grammar note: Remember to change words according to gender. Use *Buongiorno, figlia mia*, if you have a daughter.

Cultural note: Between the mid 1800's and the early 1900's millions of Italian people emigrated to different parts of the world. Many resettled in the United States, but many others moved to Argentina, Brazil, Uraguay, Australia and Canada. These brave Italians spread their language, culture and customs to all different parts of the world.

Idea! Start your day in Italian! Wake your children every day with a cheery, *"Svegliati/ Svegliatevi! Buongiorno figlio mio/ Buongiorno figlia mia"*.

Week 42: Getting Ready

Review: Week 41: Wake Up!

Vocabulary:

Mi lavo il viso.   (I wash my face.)
mee-lah-voh-ihl-vee-zoh

Mi lavo i denti.   (I brush my teeth.)
mee-lah-voh-ih-dehn-tee

Mi vesto.   (I get dressed.)
mee-veh-stoh

Grammar: When we are writing or speaking about parts of the body we use the articles *il,la,i* or *le* instead of the pronoun *mio, mia, miei, mie.*

Cultural note: Italian explorers changed the world. If not for the discoveries of explorers such as Columbus and Vespucci, the world today might be a very different place.

Idea! Have your child tell you what he has to do in the morning before he leaves for school or otherwise starts his day.

Week 43: I Want To Wear.....(A)

Review: Week 42: Getting Ready

Vocabulary:

Vorrei indossare......	(I want to wear....)
Voh-rehy-indoh-sah-reh	
una maglietta	(tee shirt)
uh-nah-mah-lyeh-tah	
i pantaloni	(pants)
ih-pahn-tah-loh-nee	
un vestito	(dress)
uhn-veh-stee-toh	
una gonna	(skirt)
uh-nah-goh-nah	
i pantaloncini	(shorts)
ih-pahn-tah-lohn-chee-nee	

Grammar note: Remember number agreement. You must match your pronoun or article to your noun.

Cultural note: People of Italian birth and descent have had a profound impact on the culture and development of the United States. Italians fought in the Revolutionary War, helped build the railroad system, bridges, dams and highways, created colleges and universities, shaped American sports and contributed to the development of arts and sciences.

Idea! Before you put your kids to bed, help them pick out their outfits using their Italian vocabulary.

Week 44: I Want To Wear ...(B)

Review: Week 43: I Want To Wear....(A)

Vocabulary:

il rosa *ihl-roh-zah*	(pink)
il rosso *ihl-roh-soh*	(red)
il blu *ihl-blue*	(blue)
il verde *ihl-vehr-deh*	(green)
il bianco *ihl-byahn-koh*	(white)
il nero *ihl-neh-roh*	(black)
l'arancione *lah-rahn-choh-neh*	(orange)
il giallo *ihl-jah-loh*	(yellow)
il viola *ihl-vyoh-lah*	(purple)

Grammar note: The words for some colors in Italian have different endings when they are used with a masculine or a feminine noun.

For example:

> Una gonna nera – A black skirt

> Un vestito nero – A black dress

Cultural note: Some of baseball's heroes are of Italian descent. Joe DiMaggio, Yogi Berra, Tommy Lasorda and Joe Torre are just a few famous Italian American baseball greats.

Idea! Play *I Spy* using your new color words. Of course, when we are studying Italian we don't play *I Spy* we play *Io vedo qualcosa*.... (I see something…).

Week 45: Where Are Your Shoes?

Review: Week 44: I Want To Wear…(B).

Vocabulary:

> Dove sono le tue scarpe? (Where are your shoes?)
> *doh-veh-soh-noh-leh-two-eh-skahr-peh*

> Eccole! (Here they are!)
> *eh-koh-leh*

Grammar note: Use *Dov'è* - Where is? for singular.

For example: *Dov'è la mia maglietta nera?* Where is my black tee shirt?

Cultural note: The Roman Catholic Church is centered around Vatican City in Rome. Millions of people around the world look to the Vatican as a center of spiritual leadership.

Idea! Hide some everyday items and make the phrase, *Dove sono..?* the start of a treasure hunt!

Week 46: Let's Hurry Up!

Review: Weeks 2 and 6: Greetings

Vocabulary:

Sbrigati!   (Let's hurry up!)
Zbree-gah-tee

Grammar note: *Sbrigati!* is used when you are talking to one person. If you need to hustle your whole family out the door, say, *Sbrigatevi*! *(zbree-gah-teh-vee)*!

Cultural note: Italian is not just spoken in Italy. It is an official language in Switzerland, San Marino and the Vatican City. It is spoken in France, Malta and Eastern European countries as well. There are even countries in Africa where people speak Italian.

Idea! Give each child a turn to sound the morning alarm. Let them announce, *Sbrigatevi!* Maybe it will help get you out of the house on time!

Week 47: Have a Good Day!

Review: Week 46: It's Time to Go!

Vocabulary:

> Buongiorno!   (Have a nice day!)
> *Buh-ohn-johr-noh*

Pronunciaton note: The Italian "g"(in front of vowels i and e) is pronounced like the English "j".

Cultural note: Roman architecture can be viewed in buildings all over the world, like the U.S. Congress building in the United States or Admiralty Arch in Great Britain.

Idea! Find a Italian restaurant and get lunch. Make sure to wish the waiter, " *Buongiorno!*".

Week 48: Review

- Review all the vocabulary and concepts from the past weeks.

  - Incorporate your new vocabulary when getting
  - dressed every day.
  - Pretend! Play puppets, paper dolls or Barbies with your kids and use your Italian vocabulary to get them dressed.
  - Label clothing you see in stores when you are out
  - shopping.

- Learn more about Italian culture around the world!

  - Make a book out of the flags of Italian influenced countries
  - Listen to some Italian music. There are many varieties!
  - "Pin" a map! Get a world map, and help your child put a pushpin into all the countries where Italian is spoken around the world.
  - Go to a San Gennaro Feast if there is one in your local community.
  - Google images of the majestic Alps, the mountain range that separates Italy from some if its northern neighbors.

Unit 7: A Few Odds and Ends

Week 49: Things Around the House

Review: Vocabulary from Weeks 41-47

Vocabulary:

il letto *ihl- leh-toh*	(bed)
la poltrona *lah- pohl-troh-nah*	(sofa)
la lampada *lah-lahm-pah-dah*	(lamp)
il telefono *ihl- teh-leh-foh-noh*	(telephone)
il computer *ihl-kohm-pyuh-tehr*	(computer)

Pronunciation note: In Italian there is no "ph" (like in telephone), but the simple "f".

Cultural note: Do you spin your spaghetti using a spoon? This practice did not come from Italy! In Italy, they use only a fork.

Idea! Play *¿Caldo o freddo?* (Hot or Cold?). Play the same way you would play Hot or Cold? But instead of hiding an item, you simply think of one in the room and direct your children toward it by saying *caldo* o *freddo*. (*kahl-doh* / *freh-doh*) When they find it they have to tell you what it is in Italian. Then they get a turn!

Week 50: Things in Our World.

Review: Week 21: Who Is This?

Vocabulary:

Che cosa è questo? *keh-koh-zah-eh-kweh-stoh*	(What is this?)
l'autobus *lah-uh-toh-boos*	(bus)
la macchina *lah-mah-kee-nah*	(car)
il cielo *ihl-cheh-loh*	(sky)
la strada *lah-strah-dah*	(street)
la gente *lah-jehn-teh*	(people)
il treno *ihl-treh-noh*	(train)
il fiume *ihl-few-meh*	(river)
il fiore *ihl-fyoh-reh*	(flower)
l'albero *lahl-beh-roh*	(tree)

Grammar note: If you want to say *the*, you use *il, l'* or *lo* for masculine nouns and *la* or *l'* for feminine nouns.

If you want to say *a*, you use *un* or *uno* for masculine nouns and *una* or *un'* for feminine nouns.

Example: Questo è un fiore. = It is a flower.

Questo è il fiore. = It is the flower.

Cultural note: Italy is referred to as *Bel Paese*, the "beautiful country".

Idea! Use the question, *Che cosa è questo?* to practice mixing up you articles and pronouns. Try different ways of answering the same question:

It is my car/ It is the car. *È la mia macchina./È la macchina.*

It is a train/It is the train. *È un treno./È il treno.*

Week 51: Places We Go

Review: Week 50: Things in Our World

Vocabulary:

Andiamo a (in)……. *Ahn-dyah-moh ah (in)*	(Let's go to…..)
la scuola *lah- skoo-oh-lah*	(school)
il ristorante *ihl-ree-stoh-rahn-teh*	(restaurant)
il negozio *ihl- neh-gohts-yoh*	(store)
la spiaggia *lah-sp-yah-jah*	(beach)
il parco *ihl-pahr-koh*	(park)
il cinema *ihl-chee-neh-mah*	(movies)
la banca *lah-bahn-kah*	(bank)

Grammar note: In Italian we sometimes use *a* and sometimes *in*. For example: *Andiamo a scuola*! but *Andiamo in banca*!

Cultural note: The money of Italy is the euro. A euro can be used in Italy or any other country in the European Union.

Idea! Make running errands a learning experience. Narrate where you are headed as you run around town and let your kids translate before you get there!

Week 52: Review

- Review your vocabulary from weeks 49-51.
- Have a *festa*! You did it! A year of studying a foreign language is no small feat. Plan a party for you and your children. Incorporate some of the foods and customs you have learned about over the past year. Don't be afraid to mix and match!
- Keep practicing Italian vocabulary. The more you speak, the more you will retain.
- Keep learning! Read Italian language storybooks. Listen to Italian songs and music. Eat Italian food. Hopefully you have embarked on a love affair with this new language. Keep your curiosity piqued and bring your children along for the ride!

Where Do I Go From Here?

Here you are, a year or so later with a good deal of spoken vocabulary in your pocket. What's next? That question can only be answered by you. The key to mastering any language is to continue speaking it. No amount of studying can make you fluent if you don't reach out to others and try to communicate. Continue to make learning Italian a family affair. You will always have study buddies and you will be giving your children a priceless gift. Utilize the internet to find others who are interested in practicing their Italian. Join social groups and take daily opportunities to use the Italian you have already obtained.

For more formal instruction, you can register for inexpensive courses online through any number of companies. There are many companies operating out of Italian speaking countries that offer lessons through Skype for just a few dollars a lesson.

Many libraries have audio and computer courses available to lend.

Another affordable option is to attend local community Italian courses for adult learners. Most communities offer seasonal enrichment courses, and Beginner's Italian is very often one of the choices. You may meet other people interested in learning Italian with whom you can practice.

If you are very goal oriented, or want to receive certification of some sort, you can attend classes at a community college where you live. This will certainly increase your knowledge of written

Italian. Course offerings vary and usually don't extend beyond beginner-intermediate levels. You can list the degree on your resume if you are learning Italian for professional reasons. It is also quite a personal accomplishment!

There are so many free resources available nowadays online that you can easily continue your Italian language learning on your own time. The next section outlines many free resources you can use to increase your Italian skills.

Learning Resources

All websites, smart phone applications and podcasts listed below are available for free. Books and music should be available at most local libraries.

Internet Sites

YouTube.com: We all love youtube.com for funny emails but it really is an invaluable teaching resource when you want to learn about or expose your children to different cultures.

googletranslate.com: Hit this site for quick general translations.

livemocha.com: Do you like Facebook? This site is designed to promote communication with language learners all over the world. You can email or chat with members in English or Italian. Complimentary lessons are available. You can also earn "money" towards fee based lessons by correcting the lessons of English language learners. In addition, great pictures taken by locals of foreign countries all over the world are available for viewing in the "Explore Culture" section.

digitaldialects.com: This site presents a selection of fun, engaging Italian vocabulary building games.

chillola.com: Go here for online games, worksheets, and tips for parents and educators.

Bookbox.com: Bookbox provides stories for children with both audio and text. You can choose to both hear and read the stories in Italian

Apps

MindSnacks Learn Italian has some really fun games if you want to develop your visual knowledge of the Italian language. Oral presentation of words is also included with a native accent.

iTranslate is a great feature to keep on your phone. If you want to add to your personal repertoire, or are trying to have small conversations with native speakers, you just type in the word you want to say and it gives you a translation. You can also hit an icon next to the phrase to hear it spoken with proper pronunciation.

Duolingo is an app containing great vocabulary and grammar building games. You can slow down the speed to make the words easier to understand.

Podcasts

Listening to podcasts in Italian is a great way to improve your understanding of spoken language.

mydailyphrase.com is a program presented by the Radio Lingua Network. It is a beginning course in Italian presented in short daily lessons you can listen to on the go.

learnitalianpod.com teaches Italian through well organized lessons so you can learn at your own pace.

Books

It can be challenging to find bilingual storybooks in Italian and English. Here are two great resources to help you locate books for both you and your children.

Childrensbooksonline.org: Download free online books and translations

Worldlanguage.com: A great online resource for books and products for both children and adults.

Internationalchildbook.com: Here you will find a terrific selection of children's books in English and Italian.

Music

Using CD's in the car is a great way to pump up listening comprehension.

Canzoni per bambini by Centro Raccontami is a fun selection of Italian music suitable for preschool and elementary school age kids.

Italian Songs for Kids by Language Nut contains songs easy enough for your youngest children to follow along.

Don't forget that beautiful Italian opera! Introduce your child to the soaring notes of Caruso, Vivaldi, Pavoratti and so many more!

ABOUT THE AUTHOR

Eileen Mc Aree is a teacher, writer and mother. She lives in New York with her husband, four kids and their dog, Biscuit.